12/19/03

D1473757

SKATEBOARDING

Cecilia Minden-Cupp, Ph.D.
Reading Specialist

by K. C. Kelley

Gareth Stevens Publishing
A WORLD ALMANAC EDUCATION GROUP COMPANY

Please visit our web site at: **www.garethstevens.com**
For a free color catalog describing Gareth Stevens Publishing's
list of high-quality books and multimedia programs,
call 1-800-542-2595 (USA) or 1-800-387-3178 (Canada).
Gareth Stevens Publishing's fax: (414) 332-3567.

Library of Congress Cataloging-in-Publication Data

Kelley, K. C.
   Skateboarding / by K. C. Kelley.
      p. cm. — (Extreme sports: an imagination library series)
   Summary: Describes the development of the sport of skateboarding and some of the
skills, techniques, and personalities involved.
   Includes bibliographical references and index.
   ISBN 0-8368-3724-X (lib. bdg.)
   1. Skateboarding—Juvenile literature. [1. Skateboarding.] I. Title. II. Extreme
sports (Milwaukee, Wis.)
GV859.8.K44   2003
796.22—dc21   2003042805

First published in 2004 by
Gareth Stevens Publishing
A World Almanac Education Group Company
330 West Olive Street, Suite 100
Milwaukee, WI 53212 USA

Text: K. C. Kelley
Cover design and page layout: Tammy Gruenewald
Series editor: Carol Ryback
Manuscript and photo research: Shoreline Publishing Group LLC

Photo credits: Cover, pp. 9, 13, 17 © Sports Gallery/Al Messerschmidt; pp. 5, 19 Patty Segovia;
p. 7 Transcendental Graphics; p. 11 © Spencer Grant/Photoedit; p. 15 Ralph Clevenger; p. 21
© Allsport

Printed in the United States of America

1 2 3 4 5 6 7 8 9 07 06 05 04 03

Cover: Skating or flying?
Skateboarders can do amazing tricks
in the air — and on the ground.

TABLE OF CONTENTS

Words that appear in the glossary are printed in **boldface** type the first time they occur in the text.

SKATERS RULE!

Rolling, sliding, kicking, flipping — skateboarding is hot! Extreme skateboarders perform amazing tricks of balance and skill. They make skateboarding look smooth and easy. But beginners fall off their boards all the time, especially at first.

You should always wear safety gear, including a helmet, knee pads, and elbow pads. Wrist guards help protect your wrists and hands. Even the pros wear safety gear, dude!

Turn the page for more about the history of skateboarding, the special tricks, and the scoop on some of the top skateboarders in the world.

So skate on . . . and read on!

Wearing a helmet and elbow and knee pads, this skater is getting big air in a **skate park**. Skateboarders are both athletic and daring.

THE OLD DAYS

A hundred years ago, kids made their own skateboards by hammering roller-skate wheels to rough wooden planks.

Fifty years later, California surfers used miniature surfboards with clay wheels to "surf" on land. But the clay wheels didn't turn very easily.

Skateboards improved in the 1970s when a special plastic called **urethane** was used to make the wheels.

Soon, nearly everyone was trying the new sport. Skateboarding caught on quickly. Kids around the country joined the skateboard revolution!

Nice socks, dude! Skateboard fashions as well as equipment have changed a lot since the early days.

THE BOARD

The size of the skateboard you use depends on your size and your skills. Boards are made of wood, high-impact plastic, or a **composite**.

Skateboard wheels come in a variety of sizes and hardnesses. Skateboarders switch their wheels according to the different riding surfaces, or **terrain**.

Metal parts that attach the wheels to boards are called **trucks**. Certain parts of the trucks control the way the board turns. Skateboarders can adjust trucks so they turn easily for more speed or turn harder for more control during tricks.

As this skateboarder takes a breather between runs at a competition, you can easily see the trucks on his skateboard. His safety gear includes a helmet, knee pads, and elbow pads.

THE SKILLS

Skateboarding looks easy, but it takes practice and good balance. Most riders put their left foot in front. (A right foot forward is called riding "goofy.")

Start rolling by pushing off with your back foot. Keep your arms in line with the board and bend your knees slightly. Shift your body weight to steer.

Stop by dragging your foot or hopping off the board. You can also do a **kick-turn**: kick down with your back foot to drag the tail of the board and make the front wheels pop up. Do a quick turn to stop.

This skateboarder concentrates on his next trick. What safety gear do you think he is missing?

DOIN' TRICKS

Try these eye-catching skateboard tricks:

Ollie: kick down on the back of the board to lift the front wheels. Shift your body to level the board as all four wheels leave the ground. Land on the board with both feet.

Kick-flip: kick down on the board to make it spin lengthwise before landing on it.

Grind: balance on your trucks with the wheels on either side of a curb, railing, or another **obstacle**.

Ask your friends about other tricks. Visit web sites and watch videos. Or invent your own tricks!

12

All four wheels are off the ground when you do an ollie. Learn this basic move so that you can do other skateboarding tricks.

SKATE PARKS

The first skate parks were in empty swimming pools. The sloped sides and smooth concrete were perfect for great rides.

As skateboarding became more popular, skate parks started popping up in cities all over the country. The best skate parks have ramps, tubes, slopes, slides, bowls, and **half-pipes**.

Most skate parks require skaters to wear safety gear and skate responsibly.

Look for a skate park near you to learn, practice, and perfect your best tricks.

Skaters' Point in Santa Barbara is one of many skate parks in California. Because of its beachside location, many Skaters' Point skateboarders eventually try surfing.

VERT!

Extreme skateboarders love **"vert"** skating. "Vert" is short for vertical, which means straight up and down — just like the sides of the half-pipes, skating ramps, and other skating structures.

Vert skaters "drop in" from the top of one of the sides. Their speed helps them catch air above the "lip" — or edge — of the other side so they can do high-flying tricks.

Pro "vert" star Bob Burnquist practices on a private 123-foot (37.5-meter) half-pipe in his backyard. Like many pros, he creates new, daring skateboard tricks.

"I try to do things I've never seen before," he says.

Sometimes vert skateboarders fly above the edge of the lip before they drop back into the ramp.

STREET SKATING

Street skaters skate on anything they can get their wheels on. They leap up to ride down stair railings. They ollie over obstacles. They even **slalom** between parking meters.

Many cities don't allow street skating. So some street skaters do their stuff while watching for the police. This is a dangerous situation for everyone.

Official competitions like the X Games or Gravity Games let skaters show off their street-skating skills and tricks legally and safely. Spectators watch the best street skaters compete on a special course designed to include many of the obstacles found on city streets.

Organized competitions often feature a street-skating course. Skateboarders combine their athletic abilities with creativity for great street-skating runs.

SKATEBOARDING SUPERSTARS

Tony Hawk is probably the most famous skateboarder ever. He invented many tricks and was also the first skater to pull a "900." For that trick, Hawk spins around in a circle two-and-a-half times in the air before landing on his board.

(The trick is called that because a circle has 360 degrees, and 360 x 2.5 = 900.)

Other top skateboarders include Andy McDonald, Bob Burnquist, Elissa Steamer, Vanessa Torres, CaraBeth Burnside, Kerry Getz, and Danny Way.

Who knows? Maybe when we **update** this book, you'll be one of the superstars!

Tony Hawk is the "king" of skateboarding. He invented dozens of tricks and helped make skateboarding an international sport.

MORE TO READ AND VIEW

Books (Nonfiction)   *For the Love of Skateboarding. For the Love of Sports* (series).
Rennay Craats, editor (Weigl)
History of Skateboarding: From the Backyard to the Big Time.
Michael Martin (Capstone)
One Wild Ride: The Life of Skateboarding Superstar Tony Hawk.
Mark Stewart (Millbrook)
Skateboarding. Action Sports (series).
Marilyn Gould, Tony Will-Harris (Capstone)
Skateboarding Greats: Champs of the Ramps.
Angie Peterson Kaelberer (Capstone)
Skateboarding in Action. Sports in Action (series).
Bobbie Kalman, John Crossingham, (Crabtree)
Tony Hawk: Professional Skateboarder. Tony Hawk,
Sean Mortimer (contributor) (Regan)

Books (Activity)   *Easy-to-Make Skateboards, Scooters, and Racers:*
Eleven Inexpensive Projects. William Jaber (Dover)

Books (Fiction)   *The Incredible Worlds of Wally McDoogle #21:*
Sky Surfing Skateboarder. Bill Myers (Tommy Nelson)
Skateboard Renegade. Matt Christopher
(Little, Brown & Company)
Skateboard Tough. Matt Christopher
(Little, Brown & Company)

Videos (Nonfiction)   *Streetstyle: License to Skate 1.* (Pantheon Industries)
Tony Hawk's Trick Tips, Volumes 1–3. (Redline Entertainment)

Videos (Fiction)   *MVP2: Most Vertical Primate.* (Warner Home Video)

WEB SITES

Web sites change frequently, but we believe the following web sites are going to last. You can also use good search engines, such as **Yahooligans! (www.yahooligans.com)** or **Google (www.google.com)** to find more information about skateboarding. Some keywords that will help you are: *Gravity Games, half-pipe, skate parks, skateboarding, vert, and X Games.*

library.thinkquest.org/J002968
ThinkQuest provides profiles of famous skateboarders, a history of the sport, and a diagram of various ramps.

www.exploratorium.edu/skateboarding
Watch web footage of professional skateboarders, read a glossary of terms, get an explanation of equipment, and discover the techniques behind some of skating's coolest tricks using *Exploratorium.*

www.skatelikeagirl.org
Skate Like A Girl devotes an entire web site to female skateboarding events, news, images, and personalities.

www.sikids.com/news/video/tonyhawk/ index.html
Sports Illustrated for Kids has some great video clips of skateboarding star Tony Hawk doing his favorite tricks. You can also click on *Andy Macdonald Rips the Rails* on the right under *More Videos* for more clips.

www.andymacdonald.com
At Andy Macdonald's official site, you can check out recent photos of the skateboarding star and even take a peek at the journal entries he writes on the road between competitions.

www.bam.gov/survival/play_ skateboarding.htm
Bam! includes a short article about safety tips and safety gear that every responsible skateboarder should follow. It also lists the best times and places to go skateboarding.

www.girlsskatebetter.com
This site features tips on tricks, advice on how to choose the right board, and news and events for female skaters.

www.clubtonyhawk.com
Keep track of a skateboarding superstar by visiting this site. It lists the latest information on competitions and includes articles about Tony's activities.

GLOSSARY

You can find these words on the pages listed. Reading a word in a sentence helps you understand it even better.

composite — a combination of materials. 8

grind — a trick that slides the skateboard over obstacles without touching the wheels. 12

half-pipes — large U-shaped structures used for doing tricks. 14, 16

kick-flip — a move that kicks the board into the air so that it spins lengthwise. 12

kick-turn — kicking down and turning on the back wheels so the front wheels pop up. 10

obstacle — something in the way. 12, 18

ollie — a trick that takes the skateboard completely off the ground. 12, 18

skate park — a park with ramps, tubes, and pipes built just for skateboarding. 4, 14

slalom (SLOL-um) — to weave back and forth along a zigzag course. 18

terrain — the physical features of an area, such as flats, hills, and slopes. 8

trucks — the metal parts of skateboards that attach the wheels to the board. 8, 12

update — to make current or new. 20

urethane (YOUR-a-thane) — a hard plastic used to make skateboard wheels. 6

vert — vertical; straight up and down. 16

INDEX